Maya Moore

By Jeff Savage

AMAZING ATHLETES

Lerner Publications Company • Minneapolis

Lerner Publications Company
A division of Lerner Publishing Group, Inc.
241 First Avenue North
Minneapolis, MN 55401 U.S.A.

Website address: www.lernerbooks.com

Library of Congress Cataloging-in-Publication Data

Savage, Jeff, 1961–
    Maya Moore / by Jeff Savage.
        p.   cm. — (Amazing athletes)
    Includes index.
    ISBN 978–0–7613–8637–7 (lib. bdg. : alk. paper)
    1. Moore, Maya—Juvenile literature. 2. Basketball players—United States—Biography. 3. Women basketball players—United States—Biography. I. Title.
GV884.M635S38 2012
796.323092—dc23 [B]   2011026196

Manufactured in the United States of America
1 – BP – 12/31/11

TABLE OF CONTENTS

Maya joined the Minnesota Lynx in 2011.

INSTANT WINNER

The Seattle Storm are one of the best teams in the Women's National Basketball Association (WNBA). They were the champions in 2010. They had not lost a game on their home court in almost two years.

At the other end of the court were the Minnesota Lynx. They were coming off their sixth straight losing season. Maya Moore was a **rookie** playing just her fourth WNBA game. Not many people thought the Lynx could win this 2011 contest.

Maya grabbed the **opening tip**. She moved past three Storm **defenders**. She soared to the basket for a **layup**. The Lynx had the lead. They never gave it back.

Maya jumps for a layup.

Rebekkah Brunson *(middle)* dribbles through two Seattle players.

Time after time, the Lynx stopped the Storm and kept scoring. At one point, Maya threw a perfect pass to Rebekkah Brunson. Brunson's layup made the score 22–0.

The big crowd at KeyArena in Seattle sat stunned. They knew about Maya from her college years. She was the smooth **forward** who could shoot from long range and zip passes. She could snare **rebounds** and stop the other team from scoring.

But could one player turn a bad team into a winning team? The answer was yes. Maya helped keep the Lynx in front by making two shots. Then she made another layup. The Lynx led 50–24 at halftime.

Maya made more baskets in the second half to finish the game with 14 points. The Lynx won, 81–74. It was the first home loss for the Storm in 23 games. "I'm really proud of the way we played," Maya said after the game.

Maya passes the ball to a teammate.

Maya's father, Mike Dabney (right), poses with another Rutgers University basketball player.

"Passion for the Game"

Maya April Moore was born June 11, 1989, in Jefferson City, Missouri. Her father was Mike Dabney. Dabney played basketball in college. He starred for Rutgers University in the 1976 **Final Four**. Dabney did not help raise Maya. She lived with her mother, Kathryn Moore. Kathryn played volleyball in college. "We'd do anything for each other," Maya says about her mother. "We've been through a lot of things that brought us closer."

Maya ran and ran around her apartment when she was a child. Her mother wished she would stay put. Kathryn put up a small basketball hoop on a door in the apartment. Maya shot basket after basket. "I never thought she would slam-dunk that little ball through that hoop for hours," Kathryn said.

Rebecca Lobo *(left)* and Sheryl Swoopes *(right)* played for the WNBA in 1997.

Maya's great aunt suggested that Maya try youth basketball in 1997. Maya loved to play. She gave up other sports to focus on basketball. The WNBA also began play in 1997. "That's where I got my passion for the game, watching the WNBA on TV," Maya said.

Maya was a leader on the court. She wasn't bossy. She took control and helped her teammates. She learned to be in charge by being the oldest of 10 cousins who played together growing up. "I got a chance to learn how to be a leader," said Maya.

When Maya was 11, she moved with her mother to Charlotte, North Carolina. In 2001, they moved again. This time, they ended up near Atlanta, Georgia. They were in search of the best Amateur Athletic Union (AAU) basketball program for Maya.

Maya joined the Georgia Metros of the AAU when she was 13. Maya and her mother traveled with the Metros for the next four summers. "I am so grateful to her for allowing me to start at such a young age," Maya said of her mother. Maya led the Metros to the AAU national championship all four years.

Maya's mother (right) helped Maya live out her basketball dreams.

Maya went to high school in Suwanee, Georgia, not far from the big city of Atlanta.

HARD WORKER

Maya signed up at Collins Hill High School in Suwanee, Georgia, in 2003. She was just a freshman, but she acted like a senior. Maya was the first one in the gym each day for basketball practice. She ran **sprints** by herself. She was quick to help teammates during practice and games. "No one believes me when I tell them how special that kid is," Coach Tracey Tipton said. "I'm telling you, she is too good to be true."

Maya led the Collins Hill Screaming Eagles to a winning season in 2003–2004. Her sophomore year was even better. Maya averaged nearly 18 points and eight rebounds per game. She also made a one-handed **dunk**! Maya led Collins Hill to the Georgia state title.

Maya was always the best player on her team. But she never bragged. "When people get a big head, it is a sign they are about to fall," Maya said.

To warm up before high school games, Maya and a teammate would hold shooting contests.

Maya wanted to win. "There's no reason not to compete no matter what you're playing," she said. Maya did well with her studies too. She kept a perfect 4.0 grade point average (GPA) through high school. "She's always wanted to make sure that she was one of the top students," said her mother.

Maya worked hard both on and off the court.

Maya's junior year was the best yet. In one game of the state **playoffs**, Maya had 28 points and 10 rebounds. Collins Hill beat Stephenson High, 64–49. Then Maya had 24 points and nine rebounds in a 69–52 win over Redan High. The Screaming Eagles were state champions again! Maya became only the second junior ever to win the Naismith National Girls' High School Player of the Year award.

Maya worked even harder as a senior in 2006–2007. In one game, she scored 15 points in the first quarter! In another, she scored in the final seconds to force **overtime**. Then Maya stole a pass and scored the winning basket.

Before Maya graduated from Collins Hill High, the school retired her uniform number. No future Collins Hill player will be allowed to wear No. 32.

Maya led her team to the state title game against South Gwinnett High. She had 29 points and 10 rebounds. Collins Hill won the game, 61–37. The Screaming Eagles were state champs for the third time in a row! Maya became only the second player ever to win the Naismith award twice. Collins Hill's team record in Maya's four years was 125–3.

Maya's hard work on the court and in school meant she could go to any college she wanted. It was a tough choice. Should she choose the University of Georgia in her home state? University of Tennessee coach Pat Summitt also wanted Maya. Coach Summitt is a basketball legend.

Coach Summitt of the University of Tennessee is one of college basketball's most successful coaches.

Maya chose the University of Connecticut (UConn). Coach Geno Auriemma had built the Huskies into one of the best teams in the nation. Maya thought she could learn the most from the best.

UConn coach Geno Auriemma watches a game from the side of the court.

Maya takes control of the ball during a game against Stony Brook.

Almost Perfect

It takes time for most athletes to get used to college sports. Maya is not a normal athlete. She played like a star as a freshman at the University of Connecticut in 2007–2008. Maya began her first game on the bench. She still scored a team-high 21 points. She also had 10 rebounds in the game. UConn beat Stony Brook University, 98–35. "I made sure I came out with a lot of energy," Maya said.

Maya's next game was even better. She scored 31 points against Holy Cross. She became a **starter** in her ninth game. Maya matched her season high with 31 points against Marquette University. Then she scored 29 against Louisiana State University.

Maya finished the season with 678 points. This was just 16 points short of UConn's record for a season. She became the first freshman to be named Big East **Conference** Player of the Year. Maya led the Huskies to a 36–2 record and the first Final Four in four years. UConn was finally beaten by Stanford University, 82–73. Maya did it all while earning straight A's in school.

Maya led the United States Under-19 National Team to the gold medal at the 2007 World Championships in Slovakia. She averaged 16.3 points and 6.4 rebounds.

Maya's teammates were amazed by her. "Maya wants to be the best at everything," said junior Tina Charles. "Video games, grades, who's first in the mile, you name it."

Coach Auriemma named Maya a team captain for the 2008–2009 season. "Everything she does, it just lifts everybody else up," the coach said. Maya scored 40 points against Syracuse University in a game on January 17, 2009. With these points, Maya reached the 1,000-point mark faster than anyone in UConn's history.

Maya works hard but has fun too. Before a game during the 2008–2009 season, Maya and teammate Kaili McLaren sang the national anthem on the court.

Maya and her UConn teammates celebrate after winning the national title against Louisville.

Next was the **National Collegiate Athletic Association (NCAA) tournament**. Maya scored 22 points against the University of California (Berkeley) Golden Bears. She had 25 against Arizona State University and 24 against Stanford. Then Maya scored 18 points to win the title game against the University of Louisville. She had led UConn to an unbeaten season! Maya received awards as the best player in the country. A parade was held for the team in Storrs, Connecticut. Maya got the loudest cheers.

Maya's junior year was another great season. She had 34 points and 12 rebounds in the NCAA tournament against Baylor University. She had 23 points and 11 rebounds in the title game. UConn beat Stanford, 53–47. UConn finished the 2009–2010 season with a 39–0 record.

A company did a study on Maya during the 2009–2010 season. They found that she could move her hands faster than a rattlesnake can bite.

Maya looks over the court during a 2010 game.

The Huskies entered the 2009–2010 season riding a 78-game winning streak. But **center** Tina Charles and others had graduated. "There's going to be a lot more pressure on Maya," Coach Auriemma said. People wondered how Maya and the UConn team would cope. Against the University of Oklahoma, the ESPN TV network used a "Maya-cam." The camera followed Maya's every move.

UConn's winning streak reached a record-breaking 90 games before it ended. The Huskies lost to the University of Notre Dame in the Final Four. UConn's four-year record with Maya was 150–4.

Maya *(left)* and Amber Harris *(right)* hold up a Minnesota Lynx jersey. Both were drafted by the Lynx.

REACHING THE TOP

The Minnesota Lynx held the first pick in the 2011 WNBA **draft**. Maya was the clear choice. "It's been such a journey," Maya said after being chosen. "It's finally here. I'm excited to get started this summer."

Maya signed a **contract** with the Lynx. Later, she met with reporters at Target Center in Minneapolis, where the Lynx play. On a wall nearby was a fresh painting of Maya. An airplane with a banner that read "Welcome Maya Moore" flew over the city. She was asked what advice she could offer as a rookie. "Advice? I might not be able to speak this season," she said. "Yes, ma'am. No, ma'am. I will score for you. What do you need?" Reporters laughed. They knew Maya would have plenty of wisdom to share with her teammates.

In 2011, Maya was selected by President Barack Obama to play in a basketball game to entertain wounded U.S. soldiers. Other players included Dwyane Wade, LeBron James, Magic Johnson, and Bill Russell.

Maya drives to the basket in 2011.

Maya helped the team right away. She averaged more than 12 points in her first 27 games with Minnesota. Even better, she helped turn the Lynx into winners. The team had the best record in the WNBA and were in the playoffs.

Maya was asked if she could lead the Lynx to the **WNBA Finals**. "I go into every team that I play for expecting to win a championship," she replied. "I don't want to limit it to the playoffs. I want to win a championship."

The Lynx beat San Antonio and Phoenix to reach the WNBA Finals. Minnesota was on a roll and beat Atlanta in the Finals in three games. Maya and the Lynx were WNBA champions!

Maya holds the WNBA championship trophy.

Selected Career Highlights

2011   Led the Lynx to a WNBA championship
Named WNBA Rookie of the Year
Led the Lynx to the best regular-season record in the WNBA
Led UConn to the Final Four
Named Big East Player of the Year
Won John Wooden Award as women's college basketball
   Player of the Year
Named Associated Press First-Team All-America for the
   fourth time
Selected first in WNBA draft by the Minnesota Lynx
Became first female basketball player to sign with the
   Jordan Brand of Nike

2010   Led UConn to a national championship and an undefeated season
Led UConn in scoring with the second most points in a season (736)
Named Associated Press First-Team All-America for the third time
Won ESPY Award for Best Female College Athlete

2009   Led UConn to a national championship and an undefeated season
Set UConn single-season scoring record with 754 points
Won John Wooden Award as women's college basketball Player of
   the Year
Named Big East Player of the Year
Named Associated Press First-Team All-America for second time
Won ESPY Award for Best Female College Athlete

2008   Set UConn single-season freshman scoring record with 678 points
Led UConn to a 36–2 record
Led UConn in scoring (averaging 17.8 points per game)
Named Big East Player of the Year (first freshman, male or female,
   to win the award)
Named Associated Press First-Team All-America for the first time

2007   Led Collins Hill High School to its third straight Georgia state title
Named Naismith High School Girls' Basketball Player of the Year
Named WBCA High School All-America Game Most Valuable Player

2006   Led Collins Hill High School to second straight Georgia state title
Led Collins Hill by averaging 24 points, 11 rebounds, 5 steals, and 5
   assists
Named Naismith High School Girls' Basketball Player of the Year

2005   Led Collins Hill High School to the Georgia state title

Glossary

center: a player on a basketball team who usually plays close to the basket

conference: a group of teams. In college, there are many conferences, such as the Big East Conference and the Big Ten Conference. In the WNBA, there are two, the Eastern Conference and the Western Conference.

contract: a deal signed by a player and a team that states the amount of money the player is to be paid and the number of years the player is to play

defenders: players whose job it is to stop the other team from scoring points

draft: a yearly event in which teams take turns choosing new players from a selected group

dunk: when a player slams the basketball through the basket

Final Four: the last stage of the yearly NCAA end-of-the-season tournament, so named because only four teams remain

forward: a player on a basketball team who usually plays close to the basket. Forwards need to rebound and shoot the ball well.

layup: a shot attempted from close range

National Collegiate Athletic Association (NCAA) tournament: an end-of-the-season competition in which 64 teams play to decide the national champion of college basketball

opening tip: a play to start a basketball game in which a referee tosses the ball in the air and one player from each team jumps to tip it to a teammate

overtime: extra time played to decide the winner of a game

playoffs: a series of games held every year to decide a champion

rebounds: grabbing missed shots that bounce off the basketball hoop's backboard or rim

rookie: a first-year player

sprints: short-distance runs

starter: in basketball, one of the five players on each team who begins the game on the court

WNBA Finals: the WNBA's championship series. The team that wins three games in the series becomes the WNBA champion.

Further Reading & Websites

Kennedy, Mike, and Mark Stewart. *Swish: The Quest for Basketball's Perfect Shot*. Minneapolis: Millbrook Press, 2009.

Minnesota Lynx: The Official Site
http://www.wnba.com/lynx
The official website of the Minnesota Lynx that includes the team schedule and game results, late-breaking news, biographies of players like Maya Moore, statistics, team history, and much more.

The Official Site of the Women's National Basketball Association
http://www.wnba.com
The WNBA's official website provides fans with the latest scores, schedules, and standings, biographies and statistics of players, as well as the league's official online store.

Sports Illustrated Kids
http://www.sikids.com
The *Sports Illustrated Kids* website covers all sports, including women's basketball.

UConn Women's Basketball: The Official Site
http://www.uconnhuskies.com/sports/w-baskbl/
The official site of the University of Connecticut women's basketball program that features game results, biographies of current and former players like Maya Moore, all-time records, the upcoming schedule, and more.

Index

Photo Acknowledgments

The images in this book are used with the permission of: © Chuck Meyers/MCT via Getty Images, p. 4; © Terence Vaccaro/NBAE via Getty Images, p. 5; AP Photo/Elaine Thompson, pp. 6, 7; © CORBIS, p. 8; AP Photo/Richard Drew, p. 10; AP Photo/Jessica Hill, pp. 11, 18, 25; © Walter Bibikow/Jon Arnold Images Ltd./Alamy, p. 12; © Darrell Walker/UTHM/Icon SMI, pp. 13, 14; © Greg Drzazgowski/Icon SMI/CORBIS, p. 16; © Kelly L. Cox/Zuma Press/CORBIS, p. 17; © Brian Pohorylo/Icon SMI, pp. 21, 22; © Mike Stone/Reuters/CORBIS, p. 23; © Kelly Kline/Icon SMI, p. 24; © Jerry Holt/Minneapolis Star Tribune/ZUMA Press, p. 27; © Kevin C. Cox/Getty Images, p. 28; © David Sherman/NBAE via Getty Images, p. 29.

Front Cover: AP Photo/Paul Battaglia.

Main body text set in PMN Caecilia 16/28. Typeface provided by Linotype AG.